C0-DXE-963

Dedicated to little girls everywhere, in hopes they aspire to be more than just a princess.

- **Avani**

© 2023 by Modish LLC. All rights reserved.

No part of this book may be reproduced or transmitted in any form or by any means, electronic or mechanical, including photocopying, recording, or by any information storage and retrieval system without written permission of the author.

Arunima
SINHA

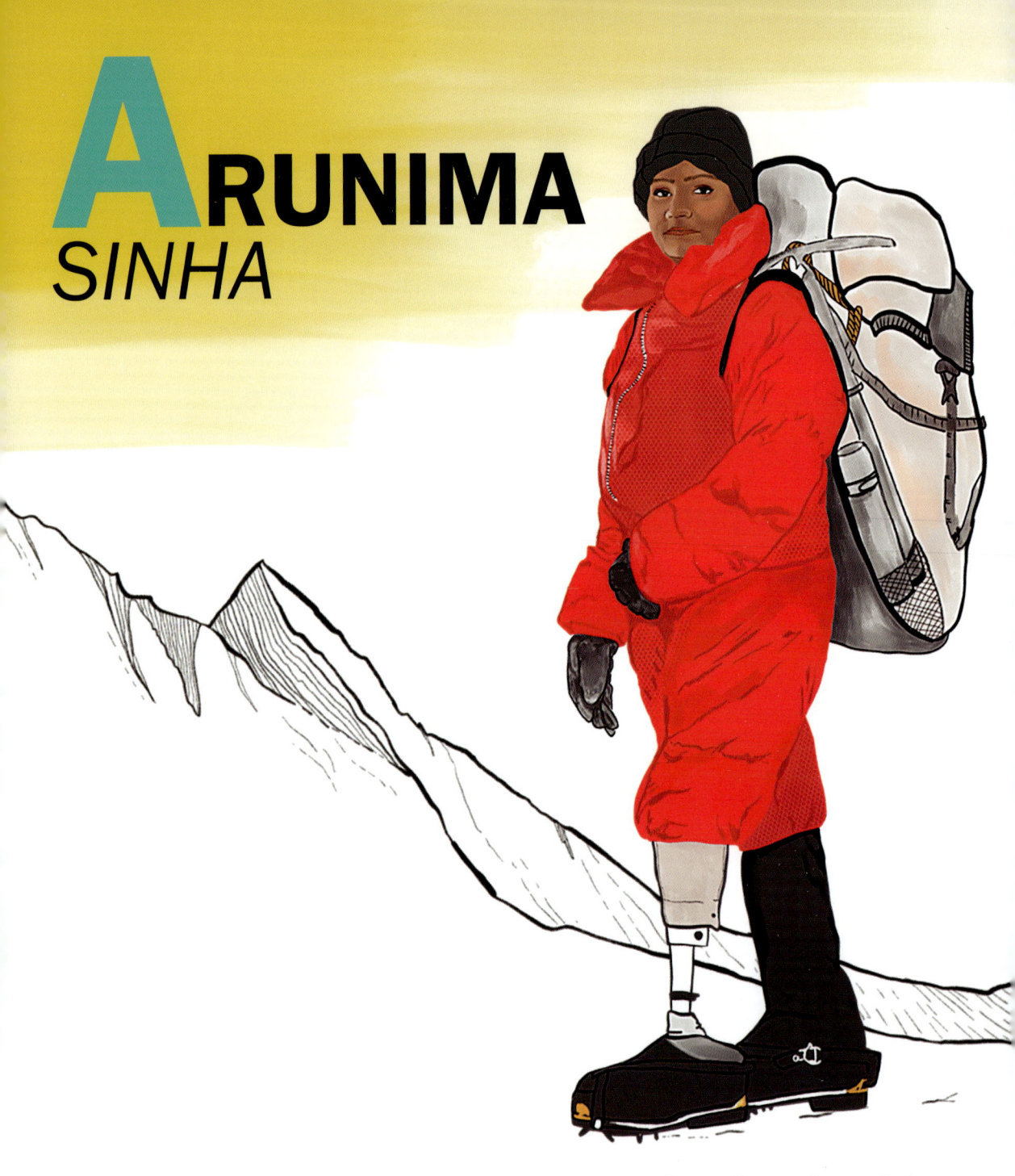

Arunima loved to play sports and **be active**. One day, while traveling on a train, she had an accident and lost one of her legs. Arunima was scared, but she decided she was going to be **strong and brave**. So, she climbed not one... not two... but seven mountains in each of the seven continents around the world.

BIMLA
BUTI

She is a **scientist** who loves to learn and make discoveries about the world around her.

Bimla inherited her **interest in math** from her father and fell even more in love with it through science. She was so passionate about her work as a **physicist** – a profession not commonly pursued by women – that she chose to never get married. Bimla is now encouraging young girls to **study math and science** through her foundation.

She is a **police officer** who helps keep India safe by catching bad guys.

When **Chayya** was a young girl, her father encouraged her to be **strong, inside and out**. She took karate lessons at a young age and decided to become a police officer.

One night, a young girl and her friend were badly hurt. Chhaya and her team cracked the case, and **caught the bad guys** to make sure they would never hurt anyone else again.

CHHAYA SHARMA

Durgavati Devi

She was a **courageous** woman who fought to make India an independent country.

Durgavati was married at the age of 11, but her marriage introduced her to a group of people who would all become close friends. Durgavati, her husband, and their friends all wanted one thing: to **make India independent** from British rule.

Years later, Durgavati resumed her **love for teaching** and opened a school.

EKTA KAPOOR

She is the **queen of storytelling** and has made hundreds of television shows and movies.

As the daughter of the famous actor, Jeetendra, **Ekta** grew up behind the camera. With the help of her mother, Ekta made her first TV show at the age of 19, and has continued to make more popular shows about Indian families and friendships ever since. She is known as the "**Queen of Indian Television**."

FALGUNI NAYAR

She built one of the largest Indian makeup companies, called Nykaa.

Falguni has never been scared to fail, which is why she took a risk and **started a new business** at the age of 50. Even though she didn't know much about selling makeup, she turned Nykaa into a household name in India within five years.

Gitanjali Rao

She is a young inventor who **loves to solve problems** using science and technology.

Gitanjali wants to make the world a happier place by solving everyday problems. Her projects have ranged from ways we can make drinking water safe to reminding kids to be kind. She believes every small act helps solve a bigger problem.

"Don't try to fix every problem, just focus on one that excites you."

She was the **first female solo pilot** in the Indian Air Force.

As the daughter of an army veteran, **Harita** wanted to be just like her father. During this time, flying army planes was thought to be too dangerous for women. But Harita wanted to prove that **girls could do anything**. Her **adventurous** spirit and **courage** helped her soar high.

HARITA
KAUR DEOL

INDRA
NOOYI

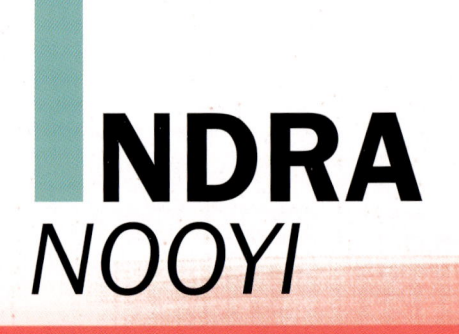

She was one of the first few women executives to **run a large global company.**

Indra's parents wanted her to get the best education, even if it meant that she would move far away to a new country.

Indra believes that women should be **treated fairly** at work and at home, and that this **equality is important** for everyone.

Jhumpa Lahiri

She is an **author** and has written many books about immigrant families.

As the daughter of a librarian and a teacher, Jhumpa's **love for books** began at a young age. Her stories are inspired by her life experiences as a Bengali raised in America.

Jhumpa won one of the highest awards for her **talented writing**.

Kamala
HARRIS

"Don't sit around and complain about things – do something."

She is the first woman and the first woman of color to be the **Vice President of the USA**.

Born to an Indian scientist and a Jamaican professor, Kamala grew up in a multicultural home. **Kamala** admired her grandfather, who taught her the importance of **equality, honesty, and fairness**.

LAXMI AGARWAL

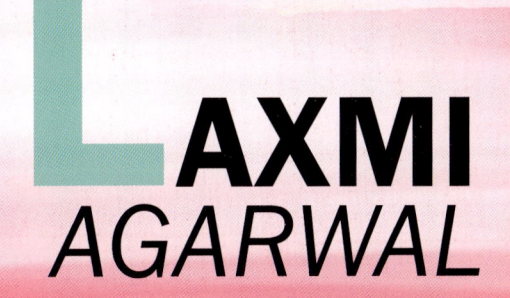

She **speaks up** and fights to **create a safe place** for women in India.

When **Laxmi** was 15 years old, she survived a painful injury that left scars on her face. Instead of feeling sad for herself, her scars gave her the strength to fight to **help others**. Her **courage** reminds us that the way we look may change over time, but that should not change the way we are seen.

Menaka Guruswamy

She is a **lawyer** who helped change old rules in India to allow everyone to **love freely**.

Menaka's mother encouraged her to go to law school, where she fell in love with the subject and its ability to help people. **Menaka**, along with her partner, Arundhati Katju, **led an important court case** to make sure that all Indians could choose to love anyone they wanted.

She is a **philanthropist** who has given her money and time to improve the lives of millions of Indians.

Nita comes from one of the richest families in the world. She is **giving back to the community** in many ways. Nita has built several schools over the years and also opened a huge cultural center to celebrate and showcase Indian fashion, music, dance, and art.

NITA AMBANI

O.V. USHA

She has written many famous poems and stories.

As a quiet child, she **learned to read** by reading the children's section of her town's local newspaper. It was her mother's love for Malayalam classical poetry that led her to begin **writing poetry** at the age of 13.

PAYAL KADAKIA

She created a huge company called ClassPass that **helps people be active**.

As a passionate Indian dancer, **Payal** was always quick on her feet. This skill proved valuable when she needed to change her original business idea. She wrote a book to teach others how to be successful by **spending their time carefully**, because it is the most valuable thing we have.

QUEEN RANI LAXMI

She was the Queen of Jhansi. When the British stole her crown and town, **she bravely fought back.**

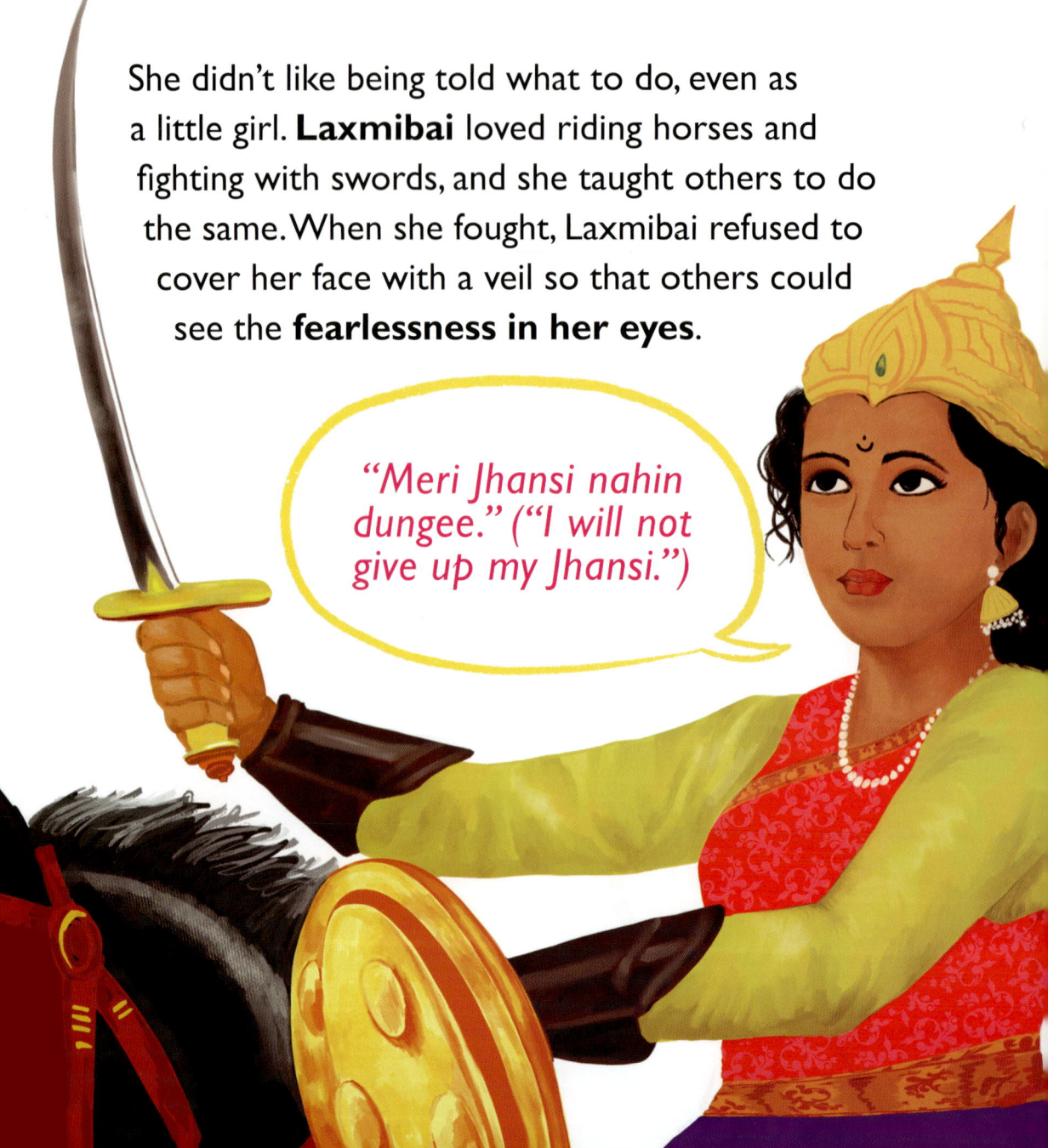

She didn't like being told what to do, even as a little girl. **Laxmibai** loved riding horses and fighting with swords, and she taught others to do the same. When she fought, Laxmibai refused to cover her face with a veil so that others could see the **fearlessness in her eyes**.

"Meri Jhansi nahin dungee." ("I will not give up my Jhansi.")

RITU KARIDHAL

She is a **scientist** and known as the "Rocket Woman of India."

Every night, **Ritu** would stare out at the stars and moon and her mind would fill with questions like, "Why does the moon's shape and size change?" Her **fascination with space** led her to become an aerospace engineer. Ritu and a team of engineers sent a satellite to Mars so that we could learn more about the planet.

She is one of the best **badminton players** in the world.

Saina's parents were both badminton champions, and watching them play is how she **fell in love with the sport**. Her mother dreamed that Saina would become an even better player than her. **Saina** did just that by becoming the first Indian to win an **Olympic medal** in badminton.

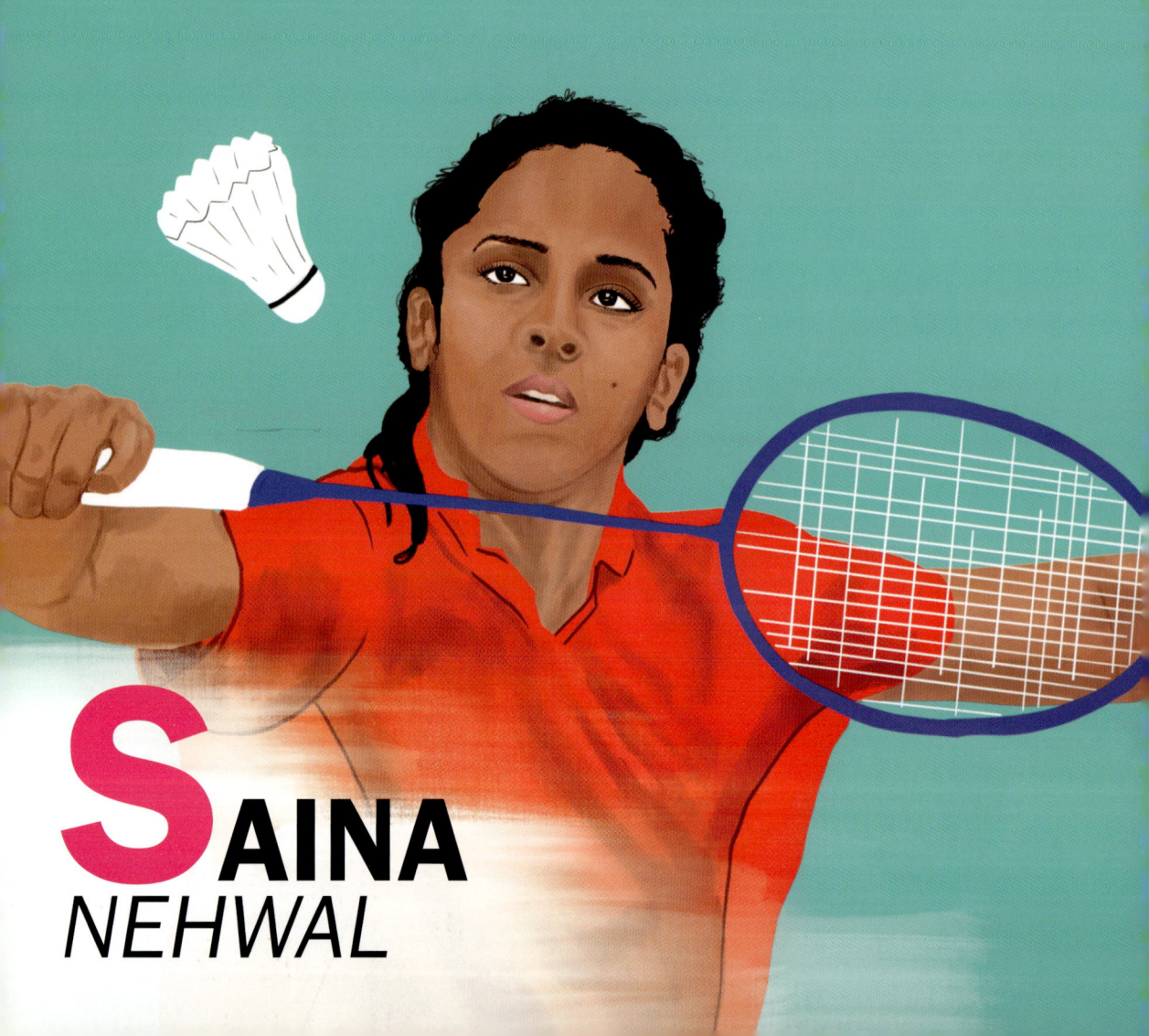

SAINA
NEHWAL

Tarla
DALAL

She was a **chef** and helped millions of people **become better cooks** with her delicious recipes.

Tarla loved **mixing flavors** from around the world to create new vegetarian recipes. She started cooking classes in her home, and they became so popular that she wrote a cookbook. Soon, a hundred more books, a TV show, and awards followed.

She runs an **organization that protects** more than 200 kids from danger in Kolkata, India.

Through her organization, **Urmi** makes sure the kids grow up to **be smart, healthy, loved, and respected**.

When she was nine years old, she saw her father get hurt when he tried to save an innocent young boy. Her parents inspired her to **always be brave and care** about others.

"What matters is not how much we do, but that we at least can do something."

URMI BASU

VERA MINDY
CHOKALINGAM

She is one of the **funniest and busiest women** in Hollywood.

As a child, **Mindy Kaling,** as she's more famously known, loved to write plays for a small, selective audience: her mom and dad. She eventually pursued a playwriting degree in university. Her comedic storytelling grew her audience to millions of viewers and has **paved the way for Indians** on and off-screen.

WAHEEDA
REHMAN

After **acting in over 40 movies**, starting at the age of 17, she is now helping the poor in India.

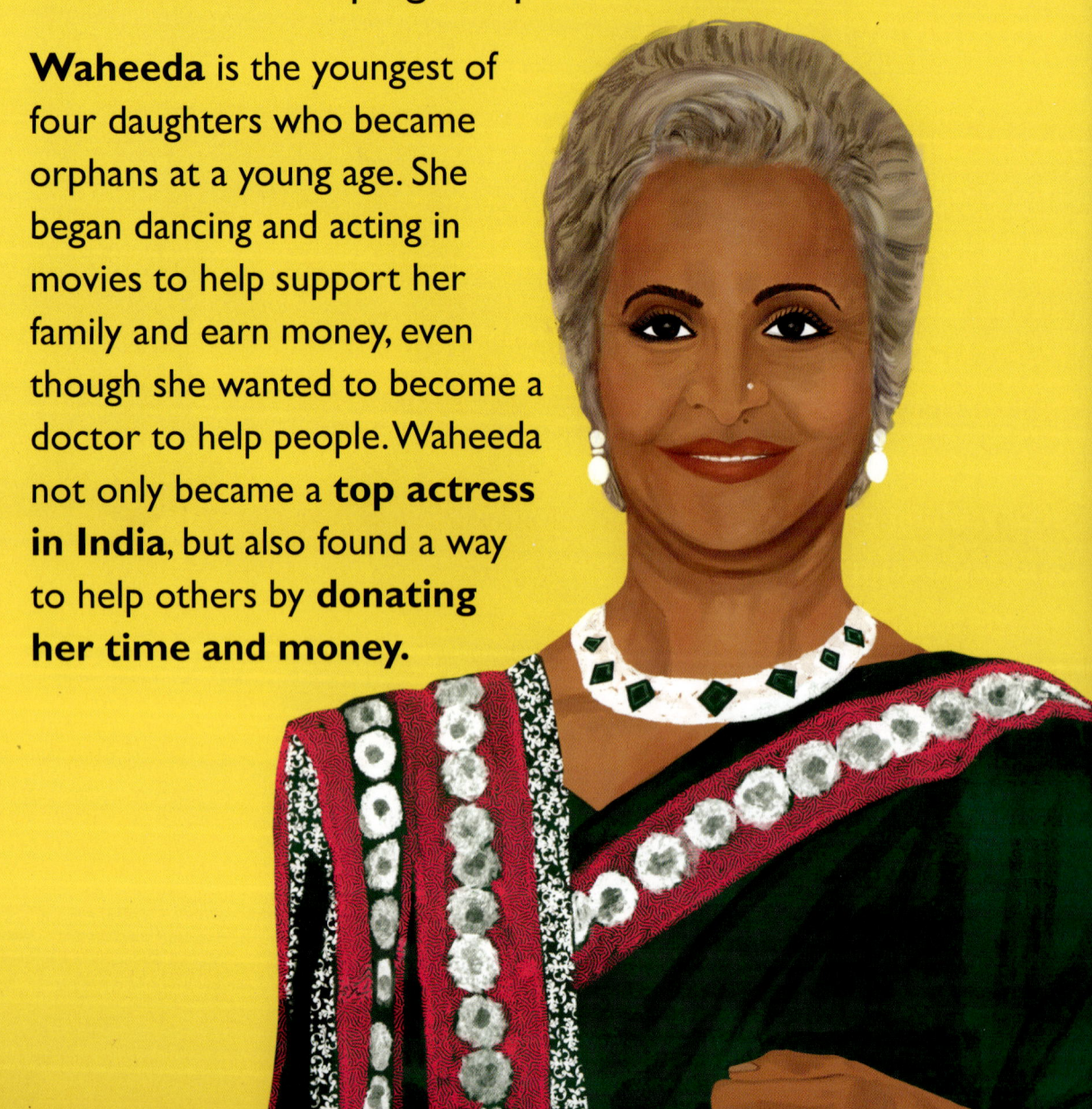

Waheeda is the youngest of four daughters who became orphans at a young age. She began dancing and acting in movies to help support her family and earn money, even though she wanted to become a doctor to help people. Waheeda not only became a **top actress in India**, but also found a way to help others by **donating her time and money**.

X

_____
print your name here

X marks the spot for the **exceptional person** you will grow up to become, and all of the **extraordinary things** you will achieve.

Yamini KRISHNAMURTHY

She is one of the most admired **classically trained dancers** in India.

Yamini began learning Bharatanatyam, a classical Indian dance, when she was just 5 years old. She also excelled in the Kuchipudi and Odissi styles of dancing. Her performances showed people around the world the **beauty of India** in a way never done before.

ZULEKHA DAUD

She helped care for patients in a country where there were not many hospitals or doctors.

Zulekha was the **first female Indian doctor** to practice in the United Arab Emirates. As a gynecologist, she delivered more than 15,000 babies, giving her the nickname Mama Zulekha. Over time, she **built several colleges and hospitals** in India and the UAE to serve even more people.

How many of these women did you know before reading this book?

Maybe all of them. Or maybe none of them.

Perhaps you learned about someone who sounds really interesting, and now you want to know more about them.
That's called **curiosity**.

While this book limited us to including only 25 women, the world is filled with thousands of inspiring women of wonder just like these. They each have a story waiting to be heard.

And if we're lucky, one day,
we'll hear yours too.

WRITE YOUR OWN STORY

Once opon a time, _____
_____
_____
_____
_____
_____
_____
_____
_____
_____
_____
_____
_____
_____
_____
_____
_____
_____
_____
_____

DRAW YOUR OWN DESI DEVI

CONNECT THE DOTS

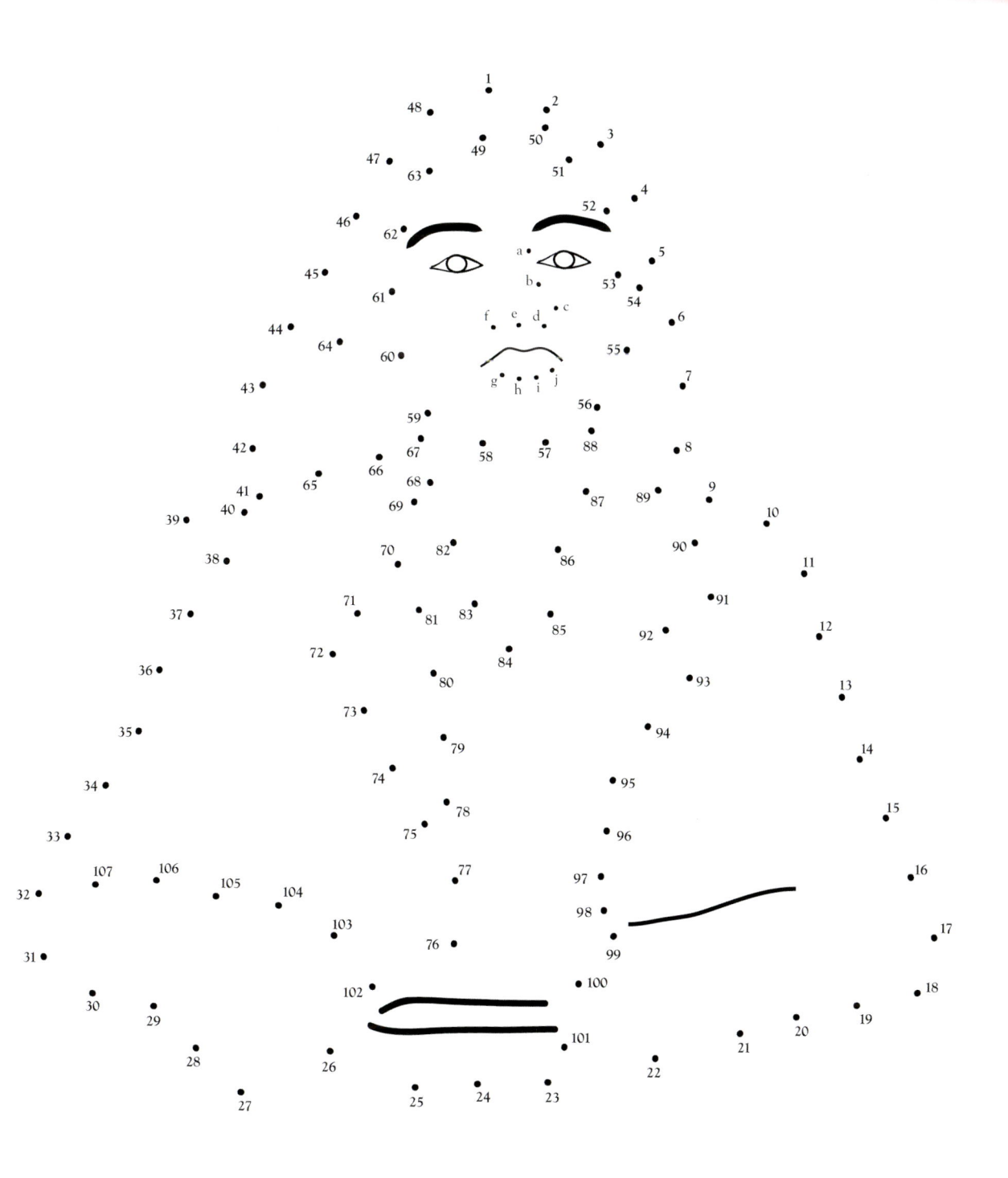

WORD SEARCH

```
U B T K A Y A M I N I J I O Z
Z P H A L Q T Q A J U B N L M
P U P T R V H P A G S S D A E
L N L G S L Z V L I H G R K N
B P I E C Q A E K T A J A S A
J A G T K D U R G A V A T I K
W Y P E A H G A U N P L C A A
T A M A B F A K V J U S N H L
L L H C K Q A V G A R A W B J
A L G E H A H L E L M I C J H
X C A M E H M M G I I N B H G
M F L Z B D A A C U Q A I U B
I H A R I T A Y L E N L M M H
Q U E E N K W T A A N I L P M
R I T U A R U N I M A S A A N
```

Gitanjali	Durgavati	Arunima	Tarla
Waheeda	Zulekha	Falguni	Nita
Kamala	Chhaya	Menaka	Ritu
Bimla	Yamini	Harita	Ekta
Saina	Jhumpa	Queen	Usha
Indra	Laxmi	Payal	Urmi
Vera			